Time Management

Increase Productivity and the Ultimate Time Management Hacks To Give You 72 hours in a Day

**By:
Rick Loftus**

Published by

42 Enterprises LLC Publishing,

All Rights Reserved,

Copyright 2016, Cincinnati, Ohio

Table of Contents

Introduction 4

Chapter 1: Time Management Basics 6

Chapter 2: Benefits of Managing Your Time 11

Chapter 3: Procrastination 16

Chapter 4: Simple Time Management Tips and Hacks 21

Chapter 5: Time Management Techniques 26

Chapter 6: Time Management Mistakes to Avoid 31

Conclusion 36

Introduction

Time is very valuable. There is so much that you can gain if you have enough time to do all the things that you want to do in life. However, so much time is spent thinking of how much time you have lost and how much work you have to do yet you do not have enough time.

For a lot of people, settinga goal is an easything but meeting that goal is always a challenge. This is because you feel that you do not have enough time to meet that goal. This is where the importance of time management is felt.

There are so many ways through which one can deal with time management issues. You can adjust your sleep time in order to create more time for your day to day activities. You can also download apps onto your PC or mobile phone in order to ensure that you know what you are supposed to do at all times. You can choose to deal with lists to ensure that everything that has to be done is done by the end of the day.

All this is easy to do but for one to actively follow time management strategies, they have to know the importance of it all. For what benefit are you managing your time? The benefits are the motivation that you need in order to keep up with time management strategies, tips and techniques.

This book has it all, to help you get started with time management for the benefits that it comes with. You have to stay focused and disciplined to effectively manage your time.

Chapter 1:
Time Management Basics

Time is one of the most important elements in life. It can go away but it can never come back, that is why it is important to know how you use your time. When it is lost, you never get to recover it. The unfortunate bit about time is that it can pass on so fast and leave you just in the same position. Time management is important to learn to ensure that you make the most of the time that you have each day.

Living in the past

A lot of people are living in the past because they have already let so much time pass by without them achieving anything in life. Living in the past is a very unhealthy habit that denies you the chance to move on in life and also the happiness that youdeserve after achieving something. Living in the pastentailstrying to evaluate what you have done in the past versus what you have not done. What happens in most cases is that you never gain any satisfaction especially if you have not achieved anything great in the past. You live wondering what you can do in order to make things better instead of forgetting about the past failures and doing something great about the present.

Living in the present

The present should be perceived as a gift to all people, because this is the time you have to make things right in your life. You may not have achieved much in the past but now that the present is here, you should be able to change all that and achieve great happiness in life.

So much can be changed in the present. If for instance you are the kind of person who is viewed as lazy and incapable of finishing a certain task, you can change all that inthe present. The present is alsothe time to try new things that you never dared to try in the past. There is a lot of time and if you are able to manage your time well, you should be able to look back in the past and see just how much you have done with your life.

Time management entails organizing yourself and planning just how you will divide the time that you have between the various activities that you want to do in a day, week, month or even a year.

Managing your time well enable you to work smart at all times.You realize that working very hard is not the way you get things done by the end of theday, but smart working is. You do not have to spendso much time working to be able to do somuch in a day. Once you plan for yourtasks well, youstart working smart and this means that you can do so much in just a short period of time.

Time managementworks wonders in times of too much work and limited time in a day or week. You plan on what to do first and what to do ata certain period of time and bythe end of the planned time, you will have accomplished it all. If you are not planning for your time, you do not get to work as effectively as youshould and this causes so much stress.

Is it easy to achieve?

Everyone has 24 hours in a day and some people are able to do so muchin those hours while others donot get toachieve anything at all. This is all because some people are able to manage their time better than the others. There arehighachievers in thislife and they are able to manage theirtime in order to function moreeffectively. With proper time management skills, techniques and tips, everyone is able to doa lot in a day to better their lives.

Time management is therefore very easy to achieve. You just have to shift your focus from working hard toworking smart in order to achieve better results every day.

Here are some of the things that come with good time management:

- A good professional reputation because of effectiveness and smartresults

- Less stress since you can do somuch in just a short period of time

- More results even when time is limited

- So much time to do a lot more, for instance personal growth

Results of not managing your time

- People who do not manage their time well are always missing the deadlines. They may lose so many opportunities in life because no one wants to work with someone who cannot deliver on the agreed period of time.

- They do not have a good workflow because they try to do everything at the same time

- The quality of their work ispoor because they are trying hard to meet deadlines instead of focusing on the quality of their work

- They have apoor professional reputation whichcan deny them a chance to grow in their profession

- They are always stressed asa result of not knowing what todo firstand what to do last. They always see the work as being excessive even when it is manageable. It takes them a long time to get started, hence the missed deadlines

Planning your work makes it seem manageable and easy to execute, and this forms an important part of time management. Iftherefore you want to work smarter, betterand to achieve more every day, time management is a skill you have to master.

Chapter 2:
Benefits of Managing Your Time

Time is always scarce and the only to ensurethat you are achieving more every day isthroughmanagingthe little timethatyouhave. Many people do not see theneedtomanage their time, because they feel that the time they have is not even enough to sit down and plan how they will work on the tasks at hand. Time management helps you take charge of the tasks assigned to you and you can get more done, with some time left for personal growth and entertainment. Time management is something that benefits different aspects of your life. Here are some of the benefits you get to enjoy:

Reduced stress

Stress affects so many people in this life. Managing your time well can reduce your tress levels significantly. Stress happens when you get some unpleasant surprises in life but since you will have more time to do more, these surprises will not stress you because you can handle them as well. Time management ensures that you have onlya few tight deadlines to deal with. Few deadlines can be met with minimal or no stress. When you plan for your work well, you do not rush from one task to the other, which also causes stress. You will not keep rushing from place to place to get things done. You are able to work on one task in one location to completion before going to the other task.

Time to do more

There is always need to do more in a day. This is how you measure how productive you can get. Time management helps you to create more time to get more done. When you plan what you need to do, you are more aware of what you have to do to finish the tasks on time. This gives you more extra time to do things which are additional to your carefully created time management list. If you have a workload and you are not sure how you can manage it, plan how to work on it and you will realize how easy and fast this can be done. This is how you are able to do it all in less time.

Free time

Time is fixed and everyone has the same amount of time to do what they have to do in a day. However, you can always make better use of your time in order to have sometime free by the end of the day to relax, to pamper yourself and also to spend with important people in your life. Everyone needs some leisuretime ina day to rejuvenate themselves and relax theirmind for the days ahead, which iswhy time management is important. You can plan for allthe tasks andstill have some time leftforthingsthat make you happy and enable you to relax.

Less effort

A lot of people believe that so much effort is needed for one to work more everyday but this is notthecase. You use moreeffort when you do not havea solid plan to finish the tasks at hand. Time management helps one to see clearlywhat theyhave to doand what it entailsso thattheycan devise ways through which they can work faster with minimal effort. Time management ismeant to makeyour work easier. In as much asyou willneed afew minutes in a day to plan for the day ahead, you will save somuch time and effort through this planning. You realize that with a good plan, you will require less efforts to finish all the tasks.

Few mistakes

Lack of a proper plan makes it hard for one to tell what they need to do first and what they should do last, so a lot ofpeople start working on all the tasks at the same time. As a result, a lotof mistakes are made and you are required to rework on some tasks in the end, which requires much of your time and energy. This is all gone once you start managing your time andplanning your tasks. You will not forget some of the tasks you need done when you plan for your time ina day. In the plan, you will incorporate all the instructions and details so that they will notbe forgotten during execution.

Few problems in life

A lot of problems that people face in life emanate from missed deadlines, procrastination and forgetting important things and dates. Not managing your time will definitely bring all these and many more issues in your life and you will always face problems. Plan for your day and prepare for everything you have to do in that day and you will face fewer issues in that day.

No regrets

Regrets come when you have wasted so much time yet you have a lot to do. People engage in idle activities other than the important tasks they ought to do in a day and when the day ends, they regret so much. Time management helps to avoid such regrets. You are able to know what to do and the time it has to be done, therefore chances that you will not finish the tasks by the end of the day are slim. No more wasted time trying to figure out what you should do next because you already have a plan.

Good reputation

People prefertoworkwith organized individuals who workefficiently and smart all the time. Proper time management cantherefore give yougreat opportunities towork for companies andemployers who value smart work as opposed to loads of work that does not add any value. Getting a good job or a promotion is easy when people are aware of how smart you work. People whomanage their time well are known tobereliable as well, which is a trait thatcanopenmore opportunities for you in life. No one will question whether youwillshow up for work or notbecause theyalready know that theycancount on you for anything.

Chapter 3: Procrastination

Procrastination is defined as the avoidance to do a certain task that is required be finished. Sometimes you find yourself pushing some important tasks aside even when they are supposed to be done in a short period of time. Many people procrastinate because they want to do the pleasurable tasks and push aside the less pleasurable ones. You will also find yourself doing the less urgent tasks when you are supposed to be doing the most urgent ones. This happens up to the last minute when the completed tasks are required, that is when you start rushing through the tasks or giving excuses just so as not to finish them.

Procrastination affects so many things in your life. You may for instance procrastinate cleaning up the house or things in the house, doing some minor repairs, seeing a doctor, completing a school assignment, doing something for a friend or a relative and soon. In the end, you start feeling guilty for not doing something you could have done a longtime ago. Other people start feeling inadequate and incapable of doing something good in life. Depression may start creeping in too, especially if you are continually postponing important things in life. Feelings of self-doubt also start coming up and you may never find yourself good enough for anything.

Why do people procrastinate?

Procrastination is a big problem for the real procrastinators because it is something that they do not really know how not to do. It is not an option that they have to take, because to them, they would not procrastinate if they had a choice.

Procrastinatorsstrive for instant gratification andthismeans that they only thinkaboutthe present.They will not think of the lessons of the past or even about the future because the main focus is on the present and what willbring satisfaction at thatinstant.

For a procrastinator, leisure activities happen all the time, even when they are not supposed to happen. He does not even get to enjoy the leisure at that time, because with the pleasure, he feels guilt, anxious and sometimes he hates himself for what he does.

How does he get things done?

There is one thing that scares the procrastinator so much and this is panic. There is a panic monster in the mind of ever procrastinator which remains dormant much of the time until the deadlines comes close, or when there is a possibility of danger or public embarrassment or some disaster of some sort. The consequences have to be great for the panic monster to come out and this is the time the procrastinators starts thinking of how to get things done.

Why is procrastination bad?

Some people do not see a problem with procrastination as long as they are getting things done. However, there are so many things about procrastination which makes it bad, and these include:

Procrastination is unpleasant

Even though a procrastinator spends much of his time doing the things that bring pleasure to him, he does not get to enjoy a satisfying and a well-deserved leisure, which only comes when you have done the things you ought to do in a good schedule. There is always the feeling that there is still so much to do, which is not fun at all. There is also no happiness in panicking the last minute when you realize that the deadline is too close.

A procrastinator achieves less

Working under panic and in just a short period of time makes it hard for one to work as effectively as they should. It is impossible to achieve much if you are a procrastinator. In the end, you are unable to achieve your full potential. What happens in the end is that you will never be happy with yourself or what you have done in the past. This is what triggers self-hate and feelings that you are not really as good as everyone else.

So many things are never done

The panic monster only strikes when the deadline for the things that the procrastinator has to do approaches but he does not experience panic when he has to do the things he wants to do in life. This means that the only things he does are those that he has to do. Other things that are meant for personal growth for instance reading a book, going to the gym and exercising are not achieved in the end. As a result, you never get to do important things that benefit you in life.

What to do

What procrastinators need to do is to learn how to achieve things in a healthy and operative manner and this means that you have to involve a plan and to get things done as per the plan.

Planning is easy, therefore this is something that a procrastinator can do so easily. You have to do the effective planning through, which involves all the details and procedures for the task to look easy to achieve so that you will not feel the need to push it aside. With effective planning, you can be sure that you will be up for success in the long run.

The reason why many peopleprocrastinate is because a task seems too hard to accomplish but with effective planning, you will see how simple and easy to do the task is, and this will make it easy for you to get started.

Planning will help you determine the priority task that needs immediate accomplishment and you can tell the order at which you are supposed to finish the tasks. With a winner at hand, getting started is easy and once you start, it becomes hard to stop until everything is done.

An intimidating task looks easier and manageable once it has been broken down during planning and this is just what a procrastinator needs in order to get started on the task.

Chapter 4:
Simple Time Management Tips and Hacks

It is very easy for one to tell if they are good time mangers or not. If you are always punctual, and on time in delivering your tasks, you probably plan for your time really well. If on the other hand you are always late, you probably need some time management lessons and tips. It is important for everyone to learn how to finish things within the stipulated time, however much work they have on their hands. The way that you manage your time matters a lot because this is what determines if things are done on time and well intheend or not.Here are some of thebest time management tips and hacks that can help you become a better time manager:

Come up with a daily plan

You need to plan for your day before it starts. This is the only way you will know what you have to do at certain times of the day to avoid idling about and wasting so much time as a result. A lot of people plan for their day the night before or early in the morning, which is a good time. With a plan, you can tell how your day will be like even before it actually starts. What you do during the day is to try to stick to the plan as much as possible. If something comes up in the course of the day, it becomes easy to accommodate it in the plan.

Get an organizer

If you want to stay on top of things at all times, you will need an organizer. A lot of people will not accomplish much if they have not organized theirlife. You need to organizeyour to-do-lists properly,yourprojects and anything significantthat willcomeupin life. With an organizer, it is easy to tell what you have already done and what you have not done so that you will know what more is needed for you to be done with a certain task.

Give a time limit for each task of the day

It is important to plan for the amount of time you need to finish a certain task.Set small deadlines to ensure that you are achieving all the tasks by the end of the day. This way, you will not be tempted to waste sometime in between the tasks because this will mean that a certain task will not be done by the end of that day. This will also ensure that not even a single task is eating the time that is meant for other tasks.

Teach yourself to say 'no'

A lot of people take so much work that they cannot handle, that is why they end up stressed so much, because there was no time to finish it all. Other people allow others to take a lot of their time when they are supposed to be following up with their daily plans. You have to learn to say 'no' and this is by refusing to take more than you can handle. Say no to all forms of distractions and temptations as well. If possible, push the distractors to a later date so that you will be able to finish up with what is on your hands at that moment.

Keep your time schedule with you

Your daily plan should be with you at all times. It is easy to work with a calendar, which you can synch up on your mobile device so as to know what you ought to do at all times. When you have such a schedule close, you will never waste time doing other less important things when you have already planned for something significant on that day.

Always start your day early

There is no way you will be able to keep up with your plan if you will always be late to start your day. The last thing you want is to end up late, which is why it is important to start early. If you have an appointment for instance, be early and you will not be late. Ifyou are going to work, be early and plan for your day before the actual working starts. If you have submissions to make, do this earlier so that in case there will be changes to make, you will make them all by the deadline.

Put importance in your deadlines

Deadlines are the times you have to finish the tasks. These have to be emphasized on so that you will see their seriousness to ensure that you are not messing up with them. The deadlines should be very clear. Mark them off on your calendar and plan and ensure that you know them by heart by the time you are starting your day.

Have a watch or a clock close at all times

When you are trying to manage time in between tasks, the last thing you want is to lose track of time. You do not want to give one task so much time at the expense of all the others. That is why you have to time yourself well to ensure that each task is allocated enough time for good results in the end. You need to be aware of time at all times, which is why you need a good watch or clock placed strategically to where you are working from so that you can constantly see how much time you have left to finish that task.

Keep off all forms of distractions

Distractions will make it hard for you to focus, which is important when you are trying to beat a deadline. You have to identify some of the distractors that prevent you from working effectively so that you will get rid of them all. Some of the common distractions you should be aware of are messages on the phone,

phone calls, people coming in and out of the office, a colleague who has so much to say in between the working hours and so on. Switch off your chats and only turn them on when you are on your break or after work. Separate yourself from people who will not allow you to work as effectively as you should. Switch off your phone if you keep receiving personal calls when you are working.

Chapter 5:
Time Management Techniques

In business, time is considered as money. That is why it is important to maximize your day in order to maximize everyday output. Many times managing time will not be easy especially if there is so much to do and just a few hours to do them all. However, there are steps that you can take in order to make the most out of every panicky day that is probably time pressured and this is what will help you turn every single minute of that day into something productive. Wasting time is very easy and it happens without one realizing it. Everything that you do that is not on your day to day list is taking time for some of the most important things that you should be doing. That is why time management techniques are important to master by everyone so that you will avoid wasting time. Here are some of the important techniques you should start using today:

Always work with lists

Making and use of lists is one of the most common and most effective time management strategy. You need to come up with lists that make your work easy every day. Some of the lists you might consider using are:

- The day's schedule- this is the schedule that carries everything that you will have to do in a day. You need to have a daily schedule every day of your life to ensure free flow of your work and tasks.

- To-do-list- this is the list of things that you have to do in a month, week and also in a day. The list should have tasks that have been listed down in the order of priority according to their importance.

- A list of people to call- this is a very important list as well, because it includes the names and numbers of people that you have to call in a day. This ensures that you are calling on the right time and that you are not forgetting an important call. Again, you have to prioritize the names on this list too, from the most important person to call to the least important call.

- A conference planner- this should have a listofthingsthat youwill say and do in a conference or in a meeting. This ensures that you are not forgetting anything, which could prompt a call for another meeting.

Today, there are systems which helps in the making of important lists that can help you manage your time effectively.

Attend fewer meetings

If you have not realized yet, nothing much gets done in a meeting. If you want to become more productive and to spend your time wisely, you will minimize the meetings. A lot of people use meetings in order to get away from what they have to do in a day. However, for someone that wants to evaluate how much they have accomplished by the end of the day, meetings are not really helpful. You have to come up with a strategy to avoid meetings if you want to get things done. If you are heading a meeting, it means that you have to attend them. You need to come up with a strategy that will help you focus on important things, then you can summarize the meeting to be able to get on with work. If you are required to attend a meeting, you need to be smart to escape a meeting when it starts to take much of your time.

Block your time table

The trick behind this is in order to ensure that you have as little unassigned time as possible. This way, you will have more time to finish up the things that are on your schedule. If you leave out unassigned time on your time table, you will be tempted to use that time in ways that are not beneficial or in less important things while you still have so much to do in a day. Block your time for high value activities too, to ensure that no one is interfering with your schedule when you are taking care of these things. Blocking your calendar should be done in advance, even before you know what you will be doing that day, so that you will not allocate important time to things that are less important. You realize that by that time, you will have so much time on your hands for important things of the day.

Make good use of your odd-lot time

Thereis so much that can be done in those few minutes or hours that you spend doing less importantthings. Ifyou are traveling for instance, there is so much time wasted when you are waiting toboard a plane. There are important books that you can read during that time, which can benefit yourwork somuch. There are inspiration videos you can watch too. Thiscan be the best time to return calls or emails or to send important emails to clients. This can also be an important time to strategize on what needs to be donein order to better your work and productivity. It can also be the time to think of how much youhave achieved so far and to come upwith strategies thatcanhelp you work better. Think of the many minutes that you waste ina day when they can be put into good use.

Time managementrequires discipline. While everyone is out and about thinking of how they can killtheir time, you should be thinking of how much youcan achieve if you put your time in good use. Ten minutes wasted in between your schedule may not seem much but imagine how many minutes you willhave lost in a day or after a week.

Chapter 6:
Time Management Mistakes to Avoid

Not many people are able to manage their time effectively. Some of us will have to work late in order to meet a deadline. There are so many times you feel overloaded and unable to work as fast and effectively as you would want to work even with plan at hand. For many people, planning and managing their time is not important and these are the kind of people who live from one crisis to the other. Not managing your time well will bring so many problems in the end, like stress and feelings of helplessness.

There are people who feel thatthey are managingtheir time well, butthey make mistakes that sometimes arehard to identify, whichprevent them from achieving the full benefit of time management. If you have been trying so hard to manage your time but you still endup working late and under pressure, you probably are makingsome of these mistakes. Here are some of the common mistakes people make when trying to manage their time and some of the strategies that you can use in order to overcome them:

Trying to work without a to-do-list

A to-do-list is a very important everyday tool that helps you work without forgetting an important task in the course of the day. How many times have you forgotten an important piece of work that was supposed to be done? Many people forget some of the small but important tasks because they do not have this important tool. Other people have a to-do-list but they do not use it effectively. You need this tool and the tool should show a list of tasks that are supposed to be done in that day in the order of priority. Try to break down the tasks into actionable steps that are easy to execute so as not to miss the key steps and also in order not to procrastinate.

Not prioritizing

Your daily tasks are not all the same; there are those that are more important than the others. There are those that have strict deadlines and others that can be done at your pleasure but they are equally important. At times it will not be easy to prioritize especially when you are dealing with tasks that seem so important and urgent. However, you have to know what task is more important than the other and this is what will help you manage your time effectively. Consider the value of a certain task and use this to determine its position in your to-do-list.

Procrastinating

This entails putting off things that you should be doing at the moment. It is not always easy to start something especially if it seems difficult and time involving, that is why a lot of people push some tasks aside even when they are very important. In the end, you start feeling guilty that you have not started. Procrastinators do not enjoy peace of mind because they keep thinking of how to start working on the task and before they know it, time catches up with them and you end up rushing over the task, which leads to poor quality results. You have to overcome this habit if you want to manage your time well. Give yourself a small deadline when you should start on every project and ensure that you have started on it, as this is the main issue with procrastinators.

Working without goals

Goals are very important because they guide you to where you want to be ina few days, weeks, months or years to come. Everyone needs to set some personal goals that will guide them every day towards a certain target. Setting personal goals is a very important aspect of time management. It is easy to manage your time and your tasks when you know where you are supposed to be working towards. Your goals will also direct you on the most important tasks so that you will give more time to them than to those that are less important. After that, you can look back and see just how much you have done in your life.

Inability to manage distractions

Distractions take so much of your time and this can prevent you from meeting your deadlines. You may end up losing up to 2 hours in a day to distractions. Imagine how much more you could do in those hours. You have to learn to manage distractions in order to achieve yourfull potential by the end of the day. Distractions may come from emails, phone calls, chats, from colleagues and so on and these will affect the flow of your work. They will alsoprevent you from focusing on what is important, making you spendmore time on one task that could have taken justa few minutes of hours. Learn how to minimize distractions and how to deal with everyday interruptions so as to boost your level of concentration.

Taking a lot of work for the day

Many people have the problem of taking on too much work even when they know that they cannothandle it all. Theseare the people who have a problem saying no to tasks and requests from other people, and they end upwith so much work on their hands. This isthecause of stress for many people andit can kill yourdrive towork as well as affect your performance. Try not to be a micromanager as well. It is important to know that you cannot do everything alone. You need to trust someone to help you with some of the tasks so that you can handle those that you can finish by the end of the day. Taking more work than you can handle will also affect your reputation because you will always produce rushed and poor quality results.

Multitasking

This is the trick many people use in order to get on top of an overload. In as much as many people feel that it is okay, it is not the right thing to do if you want to manage your time and to produce good results in the end. Multitasking ends up taking more time because you are unable to concentrate on one task, which is important in ensuring that you are working fast. If you want to work faster and effectively, you can only work on one task at a time, in the order at which they are appearing on your list.

Working without a break

Your brain needs some time to rest and recharge, therefore working without a break forlong hours will nothelp if you want to work more andproduce high quality results. After sometime, you will be unable to focus and this will also affect the speed at which you are doing your tasks. If you want to work smart, do not try to seem busy. You only need to work smart even if you will be working for just a few hours. What matters at the end of the day is the quality of work you have produced and how much work you have done and not how long you have been working.

Conclusion

The multiplicative effects of time management is something that cannot be overlooked. Proper time management is for instance something that can help you accomplish so much in a short period of time. This is what will lead to more free time and enough time for important people and things in your life. There isa lotthat you can do once youstart saving time through time management.

You can for instance use the time for learning purposes in order tobetter yourself and your life. Today, there isalot tolearn in order to keep up with the advancing technology. People whohavesome time left after workingaretheones thatare able to master a few skills every day and this places them in a better position in their careers and socialcircles.

Proper time management helps one to achieve success in life too. All thebenefits that come with time management lead to success. Imagine being able to finish your work on time at all times and beingable to do more tasks than anyone else in your office. You are also able to take more projects because you have more time left in a day.

Time management is therefore one thing that will bring so many benefits in your life. Every benefit of time managements helps an important aspect of your life. The only thing that you have to do is get started right now and see how far you get in a short period of time.

www.ingramcontent.com/pod-product-compliance
Lightning Source LLC
Chambersburg PA
CBHW070424190526
45169CB00003B/1393